A Krystle Clear Guide
to Pageantry Success

Manifest the Crown

Krystle Bell

MANIFEST THE CROWN

Dedication

This book is dedicated to my mother, Sandra Bell, who encouraged me to enter into the world of pageantry. Your encouragement paved the way for me to take action, and the decision allowed me to discover my true purpose in life.

Acknowledgements

First and foremost, I want to thank my Heavenly Father, Jesus Christ. Thank you for giving me the ability to write my thoughts about an industry that I hold near and dear to my heart. This book would be nothing without you.

To my parents, Mack and Sandra Bell: I am the woman I am today because of your love, guidance, and discipline. Thank you for always supporting me in all of my endeavors.

To my brother, Carltavius Bell: I have always admired your carefree spirit and your ability to live a stress free life. You have taught me how to enjoy life and operate in your passion.

To my godmother, Twanna Walton: Thank you for planting the seed and encouraging me to write a book. I would not have known there was an author in me without your discernment.

To my future husband, Robert Saulsberry, Jr.: Thank you for believing in me and speaking life into me. I am blessed and grateful that God chose you to be my mate. I cannot wait to be your wife on September 30, 2017.

Bishop Freddrick Hardy, Sr. and Lady Selena Hardy: Thank you for teaching me to walk by faith and not by sight. This book was birthed from faith, and I am blessed that have I prospered physically, mentally, and spiritually under the ministry of, Faith Church in Montgomery, Alabama.

Table of Contents

Introduction:

I Am Not Your Typical Pageant Girl

"I praise you because I am fearfully and wonderfully made; your works are wonderful, I know that full well." Psalm 139:14 (NIV)

I am not your typical pageant girl. My story does not begin with a girl who had dreams of becoming the next Miss America or Miss USA. Growing up, I was a quiet, reserved child who loved reading books and making good grades. I loved reading books so much that I would take my book to my brother's baseball game and read while everyone was enjoying the game and cheering on their favorite team. I even got away with reading a book while I was on the choir stand during a church service. Yes, I am a nerd. I was most comfortable wearing t-shirts and jeans (still true today) and hair and makeup was not something that was important to me. I was content with being an academician because I knew that lifestyle would garner me much success.

I had dreams of becoming a lawyer and making lots of money. I also liked to sing and write, and I expanded my dream of becoming a singing, writing, lawyer. My plan was perfect in my eyes, but little did I know that God was working behind the scenes to orchestrate a new plan.

I first became aware of pageants as a pre-teen. My middle school, Handley Middle School, hosted the Miss Handley Middle School (HMS) Pageant. I was afforded the opportunity to perform with HMS Follies during the pageant. The HMS Follies were a group of students who served as a theatrical revue that provided the entertainment during the pageant. We would dress up from various decades and perform mini skits. That was the closest encounter I had ever had with a pageant.

My mother was the person to encourage me to compete, but I turned down her offer. Honestly, I had a negative view of the pageant industry all together. I thought pageants projected females in a negative light, and there was no way you would find me parading around on a stage in an evening gown, or better yet, a two-piece swimsuit. I guess my mother wanted me to expand my horizons and try new things, but I cared more about books than looks.

Sure, there was nothing wrong with me making straight A's and burying my head in dozens of books, but there was much more to Krystle than just intellectual ability. I needed to find balance. I needed to develop self-confidence, self-esteem, poise, and public speaking skills. I discovered this and more through competing in pageants.

Even though I initially turned down the offer to compete in a pageant, I eventually agreed to give it a try. I did not start competing in pageants until the age of 17, and the pageant that made me change my thinking about the industry was the Miss Teen of Alabama Pageant. I first became aware of this pageant when I randomly received some information in the mail regarding the pageant.

Miss Teen of Alabama is a preliminary to the Miss Teen of America Organization. I was drawn to this system because it was not a beauty competition. It is a system that awards females for outstanding academic achievements, extracurricular activities, community service, and interview skills to just name a few. Sure, I had to model an evening gown and dance in an opening number, but Miss Teen of Alabama was not your typical pageant. This system looked at the entire girl both on the inside and outside. All of the girls did not look the same or act the same. We were girls of diverse ages, races, sizes, and socioeconomic statuses.

I am pretty sure we all wanted to walk away from that experience as the winner, but we gained much than a sash and crown. Even though, I did not win the title, I won a few individual awards. I won the 17 year old Achievement Award and the Community Service Award.

Years later I became immersed in an industry where I learned to develop public speaking skills and self-confidence. I also discovered my passion and purpose in life. My life is not filled with filing amicus briefs or preparing for court trials as I had once imagined. My career is now rooted in this industry known as pageantry. My passion is empowering women and girls for success, and I accomplish this through teaching them the skills I believe are necessary in order to manifest the crown.

So why did I choose to incorporate the word, "manifest," into the title? The word *manifest* means to show or display. If you do the "real" work it takes to succeed in pageantry, in the end, a crown (whether physically or figuratively) will be revealed as a sign of your accomplishment. Remember, crowns are not always decorative pieces of precious metals or jewels. Crowns can appear in the form of service, love, and/or confidence.

My prayer is that any current or aspiring contestant who reads this book will be equipped with the knowledge and understanding it takes to manifest a crown. I am a firm believer that proper mindset, goals and knowledge, and self-confidence are powerful components in any pageantry journey.

Pageantry is similar to a sport; it takes knowledge, hard work, and discipline to achieve the desired outcome. Winning a physical crown may be the goal, but growing into the person that you are purposed to be is the ultimate crown. Now, embark on this journey so you can manifest the crown.

Chapter 1:

Shift Your Mindset

"And do not be conformed to this world, but be transformed by the renewing of your mind, that you may prove what is that good and acceptable and perfect will of God." Romans 12:2(NKJV)

In order to be successful in pageantry, you must first have a healthy mindset. The crown is first manifested in the mind before a physical crown is bestowed upon the contestant. Toxic thoughts will severely hinder your chances of winning, and no amount of makeup application, $5,000 gown, or high heels can mask the toxicity that is marinating in your mind and body. The mental garbage will eventually manifest on the outside, and it will appear in the interview and onstage. Mental torment only leads to further self-destruction.

You can improve your self-image by shifting your mindset and seeing yourself the way God sees you. If we are created in the image of God and are fearfully and wonderfully made, why create thoughts that are in direct conflict of His view of you?

This will not be accomplished overnight, and you must do the work to see results. A mindset shift can be accomplished in a number of ways.

1. **Write and recite affirmations.**
   Affirmations are positive statements. By writing and reciting affirmations, you are training your brain to believe what is already true about yourself. Some of my favorite affirmations are:

"I am created in the likeness and image of God, so other people's opinions of me have no merit."

"Beauty is me."

"I am fit, fabulous, and glamorous."

"I manifest the crown."

"I am a queen who serves her community."

"My God is pleased with me."

"There is a queen in me."

"I smile and light up a room."

"I am destined to win because I will see it through to the end."

Once you start believing what you are saying, will begin to manifest in your life.

2. **Steer clear of negative people.** Examine your social circle and stay away from negative people. If you are trying to manifest a crown, you do not need negative, toxic people speaking into your life. They will only hinder your growth and development.

3. **Feed your mind by reading positive books.** You have to feed your mind with sound teaching. If you are a woman of faith, I would suggest reading the written work of God known as The Bible. It is my go to source for scriptures on faith, peace, love, etc. If you desire more self-help books, *The Game of Life and How to Play It* by Florence Scovel Shinn and *The Secret* by Rhonda Byrne are excellent

resources. These particular books train your brain on how to vibrate to positive ideas and attract the life you desire.

4. **Examine your thoughts.** Consciously examine your thoughts and cast down any negative thoughts that try to creep into your mental space. Negative thoughts can disrupt your progress towards the crown. You have put in too much work to have it all destroyed with one or more bad thoughts.

Chapter 2:

Set Goals and Educate Yourself

"Study to shew thyself approved unto God, a workman that needeth not to be ashamed, rightly dividing the word of truth. " 2 Timothy 2:15(KJV)

Now, that you have shifted your mind, it is time to do the real work. In order to be successful in pageantry, you must know and understand how the industry operates.

Set Goals.

Every girl who enters the world of pageantry has a goal in mind. What is your goal? Do you want to gain confidence? Do you want to win a crown? With any goal, you must have an action plan in place in order to realize that goal. I will share with you a few of my pageantry goals.

- **I wanted to try something new.** As you read earlier, I initially did not have a desire to compete in pageants. I was okay with being an honor student and being involved in extracurricular activities.

Pageantry was a way for me to see if I was good at something that was not connected to my academic endeavors.

- **I wanted to promote my personal platform.** As I got older, a diagnosis of Endometriosis made me want to compete even more. I wanted to raise awareness of a disease that is often taboo to speak about as well as an illness that is rarely communicated to the public at large. I wanted to give a face to the illness, and I was able to accomplish that through pageantry.

- **I wanted to enter into the modeling industry.** As I continued to compete in pageants, I also developed an interest in modeling. I loved displaying poise and confidence especially behind the lens of a camera. Pageantry has allowed me to work with some amazing photographers, makeup artists, and modeling coaches and my modeling goal is slowly being realized.

Research and select a pageant system.

There are hundreds or maybe thousands of pageant systems in the United States and throughout the world. They range from local, state, and national competitions. As previously mentioned, know and have a clear understanding of your goals for competing.

Once you have established your goals, find a system that is in line with your goals. Everything you need to know about various pageant systems are on the World Wide Web. View websites, social media pages, and blogs to conduct your research. For example, if scholarship opportunities are your reason for competing, do a Google search for, "Pageants That Offer Scholarships." Take time to read about those systems and make a decision from the available options.

Thoroughly read everything about your system.

Reading is fundamental. I do not mean to be condescending in any way when I make this statement, but too many times contestants make the mistake of not thoroughly reading the rules and regulations of their selected system. You miss the mark when you drop the ball in this area.

Develop a relationship with the pageant director.

The pageant director is there to guide you through the pageantry process. Listen and adhere to his or her advice. Call or email the director with any questions or concerns you may have. Pageant directors are there for a reason.

Work with a pageant coach.

Pageant coaches are excellent resources to utilize while you prepare for competition. I highly recommend them especially if you are a novice competitor. Pageant coaches normally have several years of experience in the industry and have worked in multiple arenas (competition, judging, directing) in the industry so they have a vast understanding of the industry as a whole.

Many pageant coaches have fees attached to their services so if you cannot afford to hire a coach, find a former competitor who may willing to offer his or her services on a volunteer basis. If that does not work, there are pageant media sites that offer free coaching articles that will be of great benefit.

Read pageant media websites.

The industry is constantly growing and many are using technology to inform and educate others about the industry. Many systems take advantage of the social media platform, *YouTube*, by uploading clips of their competitions so you can view them at your leisure. I have even seen videos that specifically teach you how to do an evening gown walk.

Practice and practice some more.

Once you have worked with a pageant coach and studied the media websites, you must practice what you have learned. You will not know everything overnight so this will take time and effort on your part. The coach and the information is only there to guide you, it is your job to execute.

Formulate a schedule of how and when you will rehearse your areas of competition. The schedule should be custom designed to fit your needs. (See example below)

- **Interview** Ask family members or friends to conduct a mock interview for you, and practice answering interview questions in front of them. Ask for their critique so you can improve and develop confidence.
- **Evening Wear Competition** Practice walking in heels in your living room and kitchen. The more you practice walking in your heels, the more comfortable and elegant you will appear on stage.
- **On-Stage Question** Have someone write down random questions on pieces of paper, and place each individual question in a fishbowl. Practice answering the questions in front of an audience of family and friends.

Chapter 3:

Develop Self-Confidence

"Therefore do not cast away your confidence, which has great reward. For you have need of endurance, so that after you have done the will of God, you may receive the promise:"

Hebrews 10:35-36(NKJV)

As I reflect back I now understand my real reason for not competing. I did not possess self-confidence. I did not think I was pretty enough to compete successfully because I struggled with self-image issues and a lack of confidence. In order to manifest the crown, you have to believe that you are worthy of such an honor. If you do not believe in yourself, how can you convince judges to see your worth? You won't be able to convince them because they will see it all over your face and in your stage performance. You will lack poise, personality, and confidence.

Self-confidence is not something that appears in thin air. It must be developed. It must be nurtured. You must do the inner work. It may take weeks, months, or even years to develop into the confident person you hope to become. The length of the process is up to you and your willingness to make a change.

Stop the negative self-talk.

Speaking ill will of yourself and rehearsing negative thoughts will get you nowhere. It is unproductive, and it is a waste of time. Do what you have to do in order to stop this destructive behavior.

Stop the comparison game.

You are unique, and you are one of a kind. Stop comparing yourself to every other contestant. There will always be someone prettier, smarter, or more talented. That does not matter. Be the best version of you, and everything else will fall into place.

Pray.

Prayer is nothing more than conversation with your God source. Tell Him your desires, fears, strengths, and weaknesses. Give Him thanks for giving you life and being a constant source in your life. Your pageant journey would be nothing without His love and guidance. Pray your thoughts. God already knows what you are thinking because He is all knowing, but pray about them anyway. When you pray, believe that change will take place. Unbelief makes it difficult for prayer requests to be manifested into realities.

Do what makes you uncomfortable.

This industry will bring you out of your comfort zone so you must be willing to do what is necessary in order succeed. For example, if you have a fear of public speaking, give a speech in front of a crowd. Engage your listeners with a topic or platform that is near and dear to your heart. You might as well get use to this type of activity because queens are communicators.

Conclusion:

Manifest the Crown

"For those God foreknew he also predestined to be conformed to the image of his Son, that he might be the firstborn among many brothers and sisters. And those he predestined, he also called; those he called, he also justified; those he justified, he also glorified." Romans 8:29-30 (NKJV)

The road to manifesting the crown is not always smooth. There will be obstacles to overcome and lessons to learn, but it will all be for your good. The things you learn on this journey will not only be beneficial to you in your pageantry endeavors, but they will serve you well in your personal and professional life.

As you have learned in the previous chapters, in order to manifest the crown, you must do the work. First, you must shift your mindset. You must see yourself the way God sees you and feed your mind with all things positive. Second, you must set goals and educate yourself. You must have a vision for your pageantry goals and you must execute that vision. Third, you must develop self-confidence. A confident contestant is a successful contestant, and a successful contestant manifests the crown.

Know that a crown will not be delivered to you on a silver platter for you to wear for praise and show. A crown is earned through hard work. Once a crown is manifested, your work is still not done. The crown is designed for you to use it as a tool for you to be of service to others and for you to be the face of the pageant brand.

It is now time for you to live out your God given purpose. Do the work and manifest the crown. You are destined for greatness, and the world is waiting for your skills and talents.

Bonus:

The Crown of Service

"The greatest among you will be your servant."
Matthew 23:11(NIV)

And the winner is………Krystle Bell! Wow! I am both surprised and excited. I smile and walk to the center of the stage to await my accolades. I receive a crown, sash, plaque, and an impressive prize package. I take my walk and wave to my supporters. My work is now complete. Wrong answer! That is a common misconception among a lot of winners. Yes, you have put in the work prior to competition by mastering your walk, talent, and/or interview. You have even adopted a healthy lifestyle in order to obtain that perfect pageant body; however, the real work has only begun. It is time to manifest the crown of service. You were not created to just wear a crown and sash and look pretty; you were created to serve.

Serving is a rewarding experience. If you did not formulate a platform prior to competition, now is the time. You can start by brainstorming a cause or organization that that you want to advocate for. This platform can be based on personal experience or a cause that is of interest to you.

For example, my personal platform is entitled Code Yellow: An Alert on Endometriosis. I chose this platform because I was diagnosed with endometriosis in 2008, and I want to educate others so they can become proactive about their reproductive health.

Not only should you advocate and support causes that are near and dear to your heart, but you should support other causes in your community. Remember, the crown is not about you; it is what you can do for others. You should be a reflection of your pageant system and become rooted in service. Service teaches you to think of others before you think of yourself. It teaches you selfless behavior. Believe it or not, you were created to serve a purpose. That purpose should include serving others.

About The Author

Born and raised in Roanoke, Alabama, Krystle Bell is a 2007 magna cum laude graduate of Jacksonville State University with a Bachelor of Arts in Political Science and a double minor in Spanish/Business and Technical Writing. She is a 2011 graduate of Auburn University Montgomery with a Master of Public Administration with a concentration in Nonprofit Management and Leadership.

Krystle has been competing in pageants since age 17. She has experience in the areas of competition, judging, coaching, emceeing, directing, and stage management. She is the Founder and CEO of KrystleBell.com, a pageantry and lifestyle blog that serves as "Your Krystle Clear Source for All Things Pageant Related." She is also the Founder/CEO of The Glamour Effect, a pageantry/life coaching and event consulting company.

She has a passion for Endometriosis awareness, and she spends time educating others about this debilitating disease. In her spare time, Krystle enjoys singing, reading, public speaking, running, and modeling.